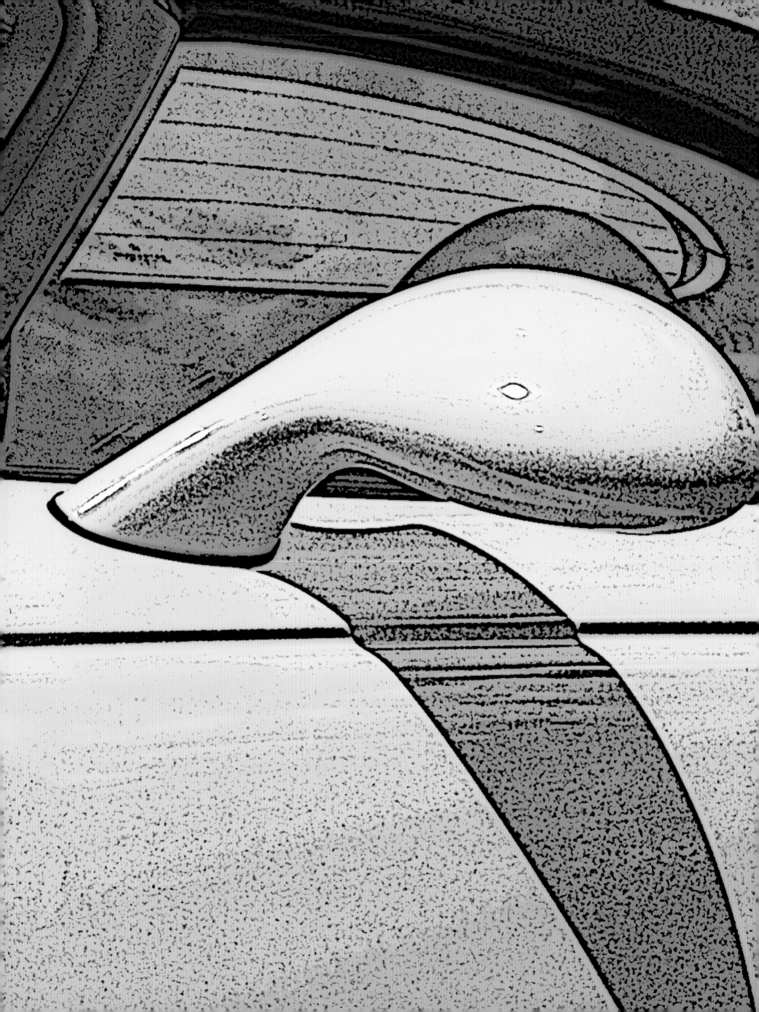

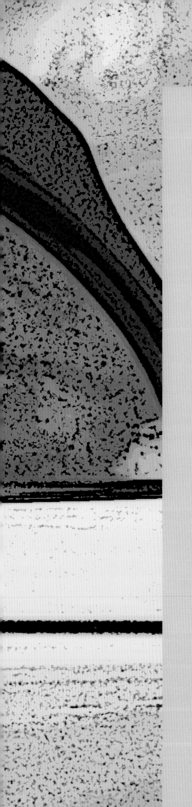

American Cars

*From the legendary Model T to
awesome modern Hot Rods*

photography by

Fredric Winkowski
Frank D. Sullivan

text by Frank D. Sullivan

This is a Parragon Publishing Book
First published in 2006

Parragon Publishing
Queen Street House
4 Queen Street
Bath BA1 1HE, UK

ISBN: 1-40547-591-9

DEDICATION ...
To all who love and are inspired by history

Printed in Thailand

Contents

Introduction

If we could just see them now as they were then; not dusty relics drowsing in dim museum galleries, but exciting, racketing machines that set American pulses racing.

Well, of course it turns out we can. A lot of Americans see their cars as just rolling appliances, igniting little more passion than a few choice words if their batteries go dead. But all over the country are many people, and we mean a lot of individuals, who are passionate indeed about their cars. They are collectors, restorers, customizers, hot-rodders, racers, and they are all historians in that they preserve the living story of America's love of the automobile. These are the folks whose cars can be found at the smaller venues, the antique car shows, the cruise-ins, small museums. They work hard but they have fun with their machines. In fact most cars are "drivers," or cars their owners drive often or in competition, and not "Trailer Queens" that get towed from venue to venue.

We don't mean to leave out the big collectors and museums; their contributions are vital. But their ability to accommodate us (and our cameras) is limited, as we prefer to shoot outdoors. Again, the smaller museums came to our rescue. These collections can contain some real gems, as you will see.

As photographers and designers, we love to be allowed to look at and take portraits of these cars. We are amazed at the level of knowledge each individual has about his or her machine; from its history, to its authenticity, to how to tease out the highest performance in those that are currently raced. Most gratifying was how proud owners were and how eager most were to aid us in our photography.

Most Americans, if they're old enough, have at least one car that they remember vividly, perhaps thinking: "I'd love to drive one of those again!" As this book shows, you can just head on over to the neighborhood strip mall on "Cruise Night," or to the next town's school playing field for their annual "Concours d'Elegance," and odds are, there the car will be, looking and sounding just as it did then.

More than a Carriage...the 1903 Cadillac

Remove all the horse-y paraphernalia at the front of a typical buggy or carriage and hide an engine under the seat. Add a tiller or wheel to steer the front wheels. A simple formula for creating an automobile; one that hundreds of Americans tried to perfect. Only a handful managed to pull off the trick. James Packard and Ransom Olds had some success with these one cylinder "runabouts" as they were called. Lesser known was an obsessive machinist named Henry Leland, but his car, named Cadillac for the French founder of Detroit, established a dynasty that thrives to this day, the second oldest US auto maker after Ford. Leland's vision was to make parts to such fine tolerances that they were interchangeable between engines, a concept familiar to arms manufacturers, but unknown in the auto business. Added dividends from this mechanical accuracy were dependability and speeded production.

This early effort by Cadillac, now known as a Model A, sports the curved sloping dash and front mounted radiator of the first year of production. Cadillac's canny salesman Bill Metzger priced the car at $750, getting orders for 2300 cars in less than a week. Though the precision that so impressed buyers of that era is not really apparent to modern eyes, the very fact that the little runabout and a few hundred of its brothers survives makes the case for its quality. This car regularly competes in back road jaunts around its rural New Jersey home. Its "Little Hercules" engine's 10 HP is enough for the toughest of hills.

Opposite page:
The gaily-decorated body-work of 1903 Cadillac is a direct carry over of carriage era practices.

Below:
The radiator view shows one of many versions of the Cadillac logo.
The rear entrance to removable "Tonneau" seats allowed passengers to enter after car was backed up to the curb.

The cast metal footrest shows the monogram of the Cadillac Automobile Company, later to become Cadillac Motor Car Company and part of General Motors.

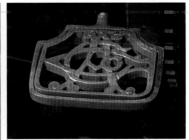

1904 Pope Teledo

Though the original white finish has faded, this racer's design shows directness and functionality, especially in details of the chain drive and control levers. To some eyes, Old #6 may seems a bit more refined than the overpowering Green Dragon.

The Thrill of Speed...

Multi-millionaire William Vanderbilt was a real racing phenomenon. Great grandson of magnate "Commodore" Cornelius Vanderbilt, he had the plutocrat's disdain for anything that interfered with his pleasures. He developed a taste for speed in Europe and raced about Newport, Rhode Island and Lake Success, New York, daring nearby villagers to stop him. Perceiving a gap between the great racing marques of Europe such as his own Mercedes "Red Devil" and American machines, he conceived of a road race for contestants from both Old World and New, to be held near his estates in Long Island. The winner would receive a cup, designed by Tiffany, and bearing Vanderbilt's image (of course).

Third place in this first race went to the Pope-Toledo, White Number 6. Driven by American Herbert Lytle, the very conservatively rated 24 HP four cylinder two-seater averaged 40 mph over about 270 miles, but was beaten by a French Panhard. This was one tough machine! It ran the last lap missing a tire on one wheel, but garnered much deserved publicity for the Ohio-based Pope Company. The racer is shown here in its original colors participating in the Centennial celebration of the 1905 races.

Another Vanderbilt competitor shown at the same event is a 1908 Simplex. The beautifully restored red Quinby-bodied machine ran in the 1909 and the 1910 Vanderbilt Cup races, the last held on Long Island. Simplex, built originally in Manhattan, was, like so many of these luxury carmakers, devoted to racing for its publicity value. The Simplex 50 with "T" head engine driving through twin chains sold for $5500 and more when new. Though Simplex built only about 250 in 5 years, they and race machines like these helped to foster the roadster phenomenon of the next decade.

1908 Simplex Speedcar

The Simplex name stood for a heady mix of horsepower and luxury. The four-cylinder engine displaced almost 600 cubic inches, more than any other American car made today.

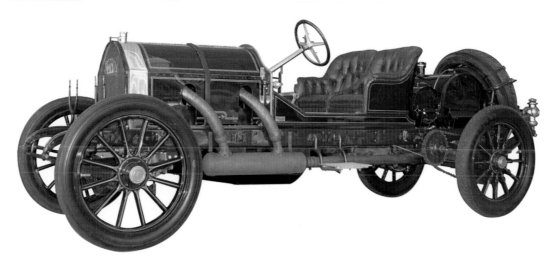

1905 Yale Model E

Many cars of this era still had right-hand drive. Rakish fenders were usually covered with patent leather. A hatch at top of hood gave access to oil and water tanks.

Reliable Enough for a Doctor...

1905 Yale Model E

A little known car built in Toledo, Ohio for less than three years, the Yale was a locally successful, popular machine. The Model E shown here, was the smallest and cheapest Yale offered in 1905, but it was a reliable, modern runabout. The front hood held only radiator, water and oil tanks, however; the two-cylinder 16 HP engine still nestled under the front seats. A bright future seemed to lie ahead for the Yale but the parent company announced at the end of the year that it was "Too busy to make cars," and Yale vanished six months later. Only eight survive today.

Brass trim would later give way to nickel plate, then chrome. Running lights were little brighter than kerosene lanterns. The simple dashboard held only a clock, wooden electrical box and the all-important Selden patent label to show car was properly license-built.

Overleaf:

1907 Reo Touring Car

Substantial cars like this one brought Reo into third place in sales in 1907, with almost 4000 sold.

1907 Reo Touring Car

Ransom E. Olds was back, using his initials to identify his new car, thus avoiding lawsuits from Oldsmobile. As shown on the next two pages, here was a car that a doctor could be proud of. A lot of car for the money—$1250—and every bit of it on show. Brass is everywhere, calling out headlights, running lights, radiator, horn and controls. Seating is nattily upholstered leather in a "King of Belgium" layout, and there is enough canvas in the folding top to rig a schooner. While the typical country doctor might not select the Reo, it would be just the thing for a prosporous big city colleague.

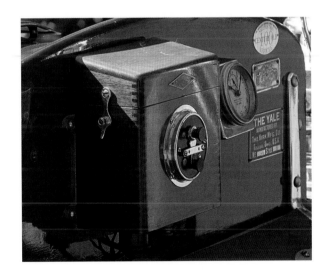

Above:

*A sporty "torpedo" body gave the
1911 Model T the appearance of a
straight line running from radiator
to rear of body. Seats were quite
low for a Ford.*

"Ten Little Miles from Town"...
the Ford Model T

"Hop in my Car!" More and more people could make that offer as the 1910s progressed. Thanks to Henry's Model T which raised the bar for every auto maker, cars were now practical, reliable and affordable. Anyone with a steady job could buy one. What we had wanted was a replacement for the horse. What we got was a new freedom, just hinted at by train and trolley. People could go anywhere they wanted when they wanted. You could visit your folks; you could sightsee; you could move out of the crowded city and drive to your job.

"Hop in my car! Heaven's not very far," goes the song from around 1920, "Just ten little miles from town." Here are some of the cars that granted freedom of the open road to the American driver, beginning with the Model T.

1911 Model T Torpedo Runabout

This is a most unusual "T." As part of a "facelift" given the 1911 cars, new models appeared. One was the Torpedo Runabout. It was sportier looking than standard Flivvers, with more rounded fenders, a longer hood, a raked steering wheel, and an exposed gas tank behind the seat, much like a racy roadster. So much for the myth of every "T" off the line being the same. But this flash of individuality was short-lived, as the Torpedo runabout lasted little over a year. When in 1913 Ford's moving assembly line began to hum, Henry's "any color as long as it is black" philosophy took hold. Though Model Ts could be had as runabouts, open touring cars, or sedans, they all had the same engine and equipment. For fifteen more years, if you wanted a sporty T, you had to put it together yourself.

Below:

Florid script of Ford logo was typical of the time. "Blue oval" came in with the Model A.

Early Model Ts came in colors. Red was available, as was green, gray, and dark blue. Brass trim eventually gave way to a painted finish.

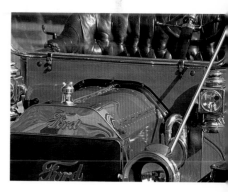

Below and right:
"Monocle" windscreen offered minimal protection to driver, yet looked quite stylish.

Whether from kits or from the factory, about 2300 of these sprightly little two-seaters were built in 1912.

1912 Metz 22 Runabout

You could build yourself a Metz car from a kit. A series of packages would arrive on your doorstep. When the first was assembled and paid for, the next would be sent, 14 packages in all, for a cost of $25 each, or $350 total. This was the Metz plan. Charles Metz, arguably the builder of the first motorcycle in the USA, made a virtue of necessity when he had to clear out a warehouse of parts he had bought from his old company, Waltham Manufacturing. The scheme was quite popular and a very nice machine could be built, exemplified by this 1912 Model 22 shown at the Northeast Classic Car Museum in Norwich, New York. It is a mini-roadster on a 90 inch wheelbase, powered by a 22 HP four.

And for the Sportsman…
Racers for Road and Track

Above:

Trim, torpedo-bodied Zinn Buick, race number 7, shown at the 2003 Burn Prevention Foundation Concours at Lehigh University.

Nothing was more daring in these years than a roadster. Slightly more civilized versions of the first decade's primitive racers, roadsters such as those built by Stutz and Mercer, Corbin and Moon, embodied power and the sporting life. Oversize engine, two bucket seats, exposed gas tank, and a couple of spare tires lined up on a simple sturdy frame—open the throttle and you were off. Playthings for the rich? Sure, but it turned out that the craving for speed reached down into every social strata. The average citizen might own a Ford, but in his dreams he drove a roadster.

1913 Zinn-Buick

When a 1913 Model 24 Buick Roadster came to grief in an accident, an amateur racer named Huey Zinn gave it new life as a racer. As a roadster the Buick had been rather sedate, with an enclosed body and an upright windshield. As rebuilt by Zinn in 1914, it sported a smoothly tapered torpedo body and lost its fenders, though the four cylinder Buick engine merely got new Zenith carburetors. The speedster survived its racing days and was restored in 1970. Huey Zinn had survived also, and was on hand to ensure its authenticity. The Zinn-Buick was one of the oldest Buicks shown when, in 2003, the Lehigh Concours d'Elegance celebrated the Buick centennial.

1919 Ford Speedster

Here's the car a would-be sportsman would cut his teeth on: a 1919 Champion-bodied Speedster. Take your dad's old 1911 or 1912 Model T down to your town's "Gasoline Alley," a place where you could soup up the old Flivver's engine and even mount a brand new body from a company like Ames or Mercury. Champion offered a new "peaked" radiator, leather-strapped hood with oversized louvers and a streamlined cowl. Bucket seats and a cylindrical gas tank completed your speedster. Color? Nothing but red or yellow would do! From machines like this sprang a whole race of hot-rods and customs. This one zips around the old airplanes at Old Rhinebeck Aerodrome in New York.

1911 Corbin Model 40

This is the real thing - an early roadster, a Corbin Model 40, and the last of its kind. Though the smaller Model 30 roadsters were tamer, with doors and an available top, this one emulates its 1910 Vanderbilt Cup-racing cousin: no doors, no windshield, nothing for the driver to hang onto but the steering wheel. Restored in the late sixties by a New Hampshire man, the car, a 40 HP four, has a trunk full of medals and awards garnered over the years.

Below:
Front view a Ford speedster on the airfield at Old Rhinebeck, New York. Note the pointed nose of the "peaked" radiator.

Overleaf:
1911 Corbin Model 40

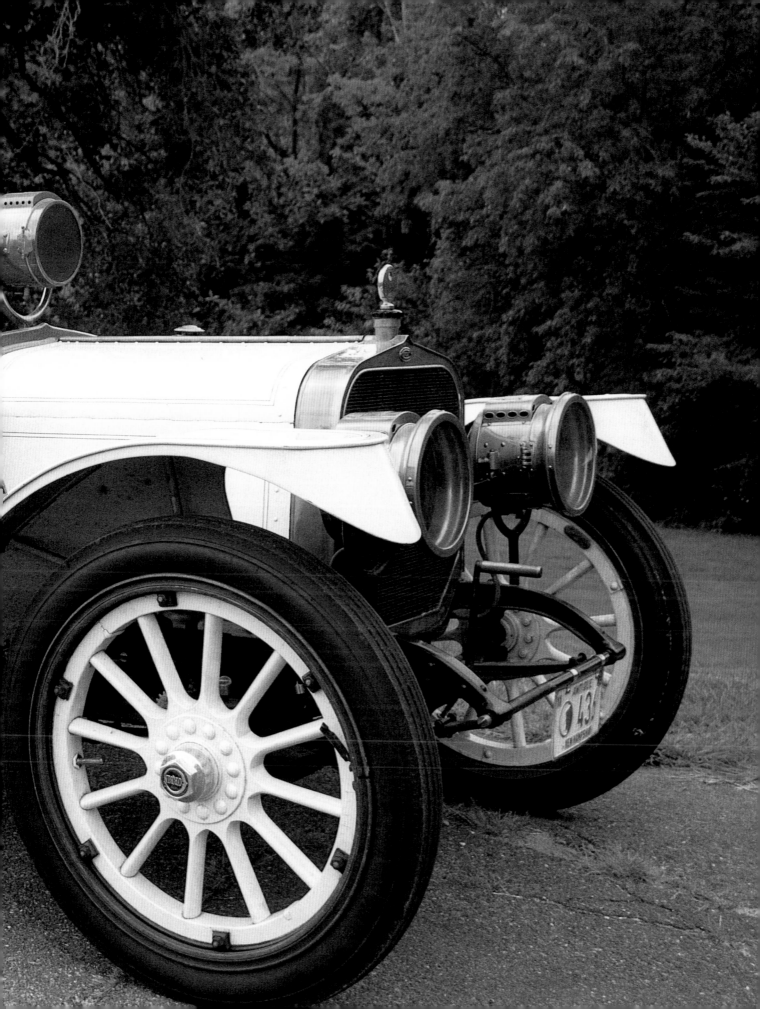

Above:
Though it was not an imposing or pretentious auto, it would be a very well-off farmer indeed who could have afforded this Cadillac Sedan.

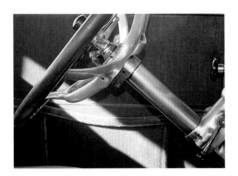

Left:
Interior of 1920 Cadillac made use of aluminum and other "high tech" alloys in assembly; also an early primitive lever-operated headlight "dimmer."

Below:
Lofty perch of driver's seat gave excellent visibility; also note that front passenger seat folded down to give access to rear seats.

A Car of Substance...1920 Cadillac Type 59 Victoria

Of course, Cadillac, its reputation growing as one of the finest of the luxury builders, had pioneered in closed cars. Their 1908 limousine was arguably the first gasoline-powered closed car to be mass-produced. This Cadillac two door Victoria sedan sold for about twice the price of the Franklin. It was as solid, substantial, and technically advanced a car as could be had in 1920. Cadillacs had state of the art V-8 engines introduced in 1914, and used many aluminum components. The body, by Fisher of course, manages to preserve the jaunty single line running from radiator to rear window that was now typical of an open car, while preserving the living room style headroom of the day. The car possesses an upright "American Gothic" look that harmonizes well with the Long Island farmhouse of its present owner.

Touring With the Finest...

Sometimes an open car was just more fun. If you were stuck in a cloudburst in your old Maxwell, you'd have tended to disagree. But, if you owned a dual-cowl Phaeton—a 5 or 7 passenger touring car—then you probably had a sedan or closed town car back home in your garage and only used the touring car when sunshine was guaranteed. Open cars of the 20s almost without exception had no side windows, so could not be made weatherproof like today's convertibles.

Even the name "touring car" has an adventurous sound. For a comparable experience today think of a speedboat ride. Wind and spray are part of the adventure. But a little adventure goes a long way. By 1929, 90% of all cars sold were closed coupes and sedans.

1923 Dodge Roadster

The middle class answer to a touring car might be a roadster like this 1923 Dodge series 116. Sure, the little two-seater might break 60 mph, and possesses a kind of upright grace, but Dodges were not style leaders and never pretended to be. We still see vestiges of a dated "ogee" cowl and bathtub-like cockpit, narrower at bottom than top. Not much of a step up from the Model T, and in fact not much changed from the original Dodge Brothers offering of 1914. It had been an exemplary car then. John and Horace Dodge, though quite wild in their personal lives, were extremely conservative in modifying their cars. This modest roadster, produced three years after the brothers' death in 1920, has a slightly raked windshield as its only concession to buyers' demands for a bit of dash and style.

Below:

One spare tire might be cutting it close for a long trip. Tire also doubled as rear bumper. Note centrally mounted taillight.

Nicely restored instrumentation is minimal but sufficient for 1923. "Salt shaker" at top is dashboard light.

Above:

*White wall tires and natural wood
artillery wheels contrast nicely with
high gloss dark finish.*

Above:

Just waiting for Gatsby to jump in and motor off. Note door for golf club storage aft of front door; also step for rumble seat access on rear fender.

28

1926 Packard Third Series Sport Roadster

Only about four years and about $4000 separate the Dodge from this Packard Six roadster, but the Packard represents a different world of motoring. Packard, luxurious if a bit stodgy in the post-WWI years, was on its way to becoming a style leader by the mid-20s. The car looks like a two-seat roadster, but inside that elongated rear deck lurks a rumble seat for two more passengers. Sometimes called mother-in-law seats, they were a fad that lasted for another ten years. This roadster's high-crowned hood and cowl and rakish belt line give it a resemblance to the sporty Jordan Playboy, a car remembered for its romantic advertising. Improved paints available this year allowed striking new color schemes that emphasized the car's lines, and the standard disk wheels set off the whole ensemble against the present-day shorefront of Hilton Head Island, South Carolina.

1930 Lincoln L Dual Windshield Phaeton

A true touring car is shown on the next pages: A 1930 Lincoln Model L Dual Windshield Phaeton. Some Phaetons had a second cowl behind the front seats to further enclose the rear passengers. Lincolns had been known as precision built luxury cars since their inception in 1920, but, under the guidance of Edsel Ford, son of Henry, they were now coming into their own as elegant, handsome machines. Coachbuilders such as Judkins, Brunn, and Le Baron proudly created special editions of the Lincoln cars of the next decade, assuring Lincoln of its place as one of the true classic marques. And the open car was always the most desirable of classics.

Left:
Almost every classic car has a step plate mounted on running board these days. This one looks original.

Below:
Virtually every Packard right up until the end carried Marque's famed red octagon hubcap marking. They were purely functional at this point, concealing messy greased wheel bearing.

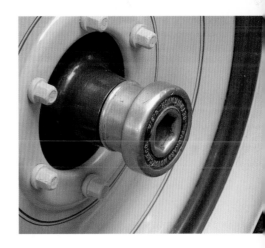

Left:

**1930 Lincoln L Dual
Windshield Phaeton**

*The quintessential
touring car. Lincolns
of this time were still
quite conservative
in their styling.
Nevertheless, twin
sidemounts and
mirrors, bold paint
scheme radiate
joie de vivre.*

Above:

*The last Model T,
upright and functional
as the barn behind it.
This car was used for
a farm delivery wagon
from 1927 to 1961.*

Henry Makes a Lady Out of Lizzie...

Songs and headlines crowed about the new Ford. Introduced in December 1927, most agreed she was indeed a "lady," but unlike the Model T—the Flivver, the Tin Lizzie—she never had a name; she was always just the Model A.

The jokes about the Model T had been getting more pointed and less funny; about Lizzie's transmission, her brakes, her herky-jerky ride. Not a joke however, was GM's upstart, the Chevrolet, an up to date, affordable, quality machine that was beginning to carve out a serious slice of the low price market.

Finally Henry capitulated. Running the company on his own now, he shut the production lines down for a seemingly eternal six months to re-tool. Suspense built and speculation and rumor spread around the country.

1927 Model T Sedan

Looking very substantial and un-flivver-like is one of the last Model T's made, a 1927 Fordor sedan. Nickel-plated headlights, grille, and bumpers give the car a prosperous solidity, which at the price of $650 seemed a remarkable bargain. In this body style the old upright windshield and upswept cowl didn't look so out of place, but under the skin was the old 20 HP four and the same oddball planetary transmission that shifted differently from any other car. Brakes were a bit iffy as well. Her present owner is very happy with his "T" since parts and expertise are still abundant, but back in the day, most people thought it was time for Mr. Ford to throw in the towel. And Henry agreed! It was time for a new Ford.

Above:

Disdainful of streamlining, this windshield is a complex mechanism providing sun visor, ventilation, and windshield wiper of sorts, as well as superb visibility.

Left:

Elegant two-piece rear bumpers were carried over virtually unchanged onto the Model A.

1930 Model A

The Model A delivered. Nothing revolutionary, just a modern successor to the T. People saw a certain familiar feeling in the newcomer that they liked. It had a flat head four like the T's, though twice as powerful. Transmission was a conventional three-speed. Folks loved that! The A's bumpers were a carryover from the T, helping make the new body more familiar. Some people even saw a "Baby Lincoln" with a near duplicate of its elder sibling's radiator grille and full crowned fenders. Of course Edsel Ford, Henry's son had seen to the Model A's pert good looks.

Pictured is the 1930 Fordor sedan, showing off the mild facelift that the A received that year. The "Baby Lincoln" resemblance grew. This car's semi-custom Murray body in a dark maroon over black finish makes for quite an elegant automobile. The current owner, a Pennsylvania man, just completed a very sympathetic restoration including brown checked interior fabric matching the original.

Above:

A single combination tail and stoplight was standard equipment on new Fords.

Right:

Delicate cowl mounted running lights were a direct carry over from Lincoln and look well against Model A's arched headlight support bar.

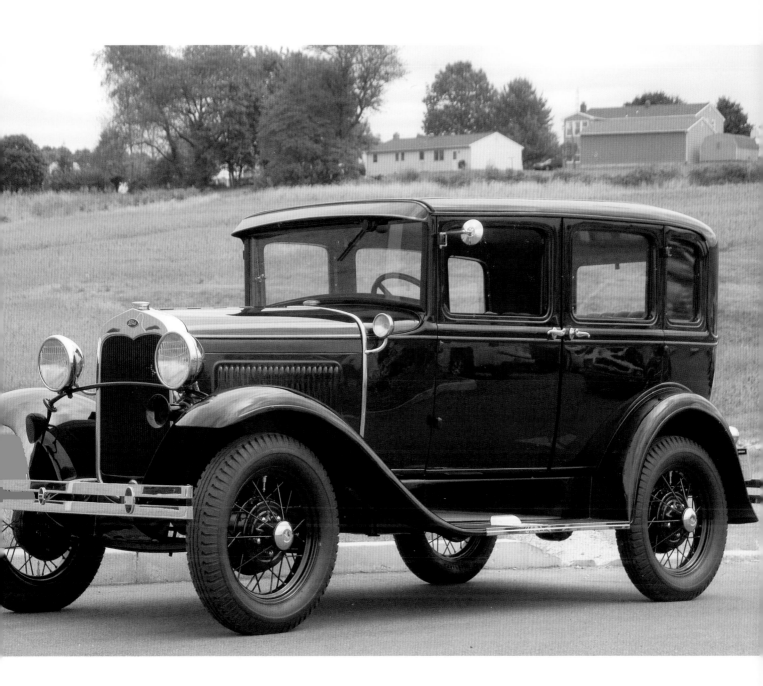

Above:
The newly restored Murray-bodied Fordor
Model A looks totally at home in the timeless
Pennsylvania farmscape.

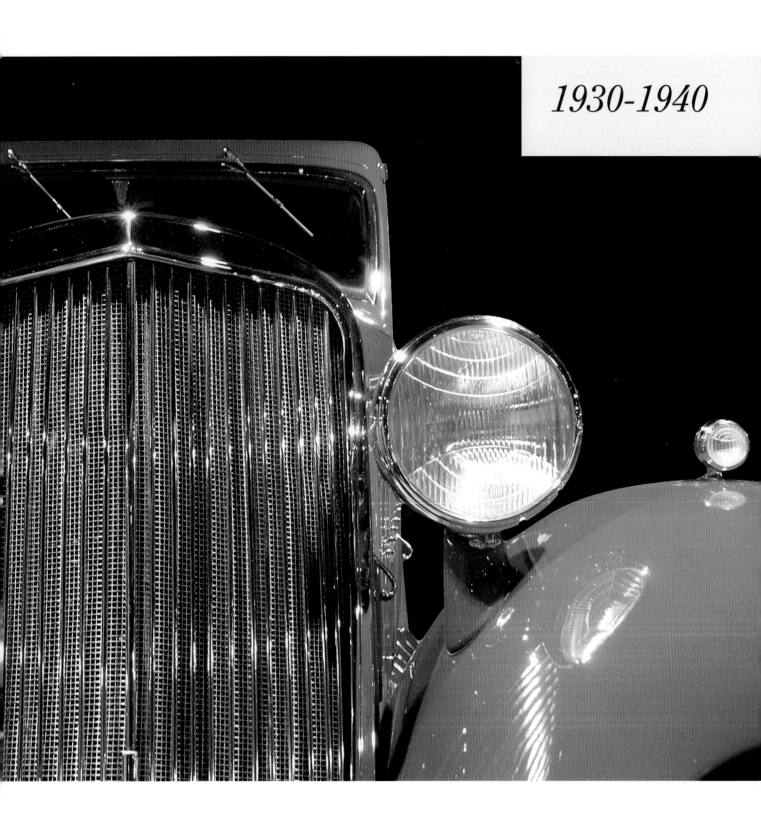

1932 Franklin Club Brougham

Franklin, the pioneer of air-cooled engines was foundering in The Great Depression. Though it too had introduced a 150 HP V-12 engine in 1932 that powers the Model 17-A Club Brougham seen here, this seemed precisely the wrong direction for Franklin to take after success with its lightweight "Airman" models endorsed by such as Charles Lindbergh. Though a wonderful looking sedan, thanks to styling by LeBaron, it was a clumsy performer that topped out at over 6000 pounds. The car now resides at the Northeast Classic Car Museum in Norwich, New York.

Opposite:

Franklin's grille hides no radiator, merely an inlet for cooling of air-cooled engine. Dealers put off by odd front end had insisted on "normal" radiator for Franklin since the 20s.

Above:

Elegant sweeping fenders and 144-inch wheelbase make sedan look ready for flight, belying its three-ton weight.

Above:
Miniscule windshield, chrome exhausts, no running board, here is a whole new vocabulary of speed.

1935 Auburn 851 Boat Tail Speedster

Going out in the finest of styles was Auburn, the car that had given E.L.Cord his start back in 1924. Best known for "boattail" speedsters like this one, a supercharged 1935 straight-eight model 851, Auburns were the height of flamboyant display. Designer Gordon Beuhrig of understated Cord 810 fame went all out, with acres of bright metal and voluptuous bodywork. They had speed to match, as attested to by the plaque mounted on every speedster's dashboard that guaranteed they had been test driven to a speed of more than 100 mph. Priced at $2250, they were actually bargain priced loss leaders for Auburn, which lost money on each one of the 146 supercharged '35 speedsters sold. The virtually unchanged 1936 Auburns were the last of their kind, as Cord's empire came undone. Christie's recently auctioned off this red roadster, an older restoration, for $145,000.

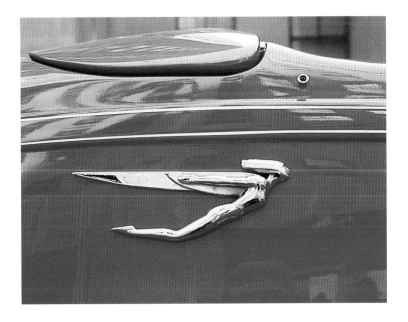

Left:
Unabashed exhibitionism continues with chrome lovelies mounted on either side of body, complementing Auburn's windblown hood ornament.

Above:
Front end of Speedster looks very business-like, but still had to be glitzed up with chrome spears on radiator.

Above:
This beautifully restored 1932 DeSoto Roadster is seen posed near a vintage barn on Honey Horn Plantation, site of Hilton Head Concours d'Elegance.

Affordable Elegance...

Above:

Tiny, watch-like, centrally mounted instruments are a strange contrast to the large no-nonsense steering wheel. Chrysler dashboards were quite similar.

Right:

Unique radiator grille of 32 DeSoto looks very much like Miller racecars of the era that tore up the track each Memorial Day. Grilles could be ordered painted or chromed.

1932 DeSoto Roadster

With so much competition in the medium priced field, did Chrysler really need another mid-priced car besides dependable Dodge? The public apparently thought so when DeSoto appeared as a 1929 model. Sales topped 80,000, a first-year record unbroken for 30 years. This '32 design was one of DeSoto's best with a rounded grille design lifted from "Indy" racecars. This restored roadster seen at Hilton Head's Concours has all kinds of extras, including trumpet horns, wire wheels, touring trunk and, of course, the obligatory rumble seat.

Above:

As metal stamping technology improved, cars could use larger panels with more extreme curvature. Plymouth had a one-piece all-steel top for 1937.

1937 Plymouth Deluxe Sedan

Third car of the "low priced three" was Plymouth, which could trace its descent not from our Pilgrim Fathers but through Chrysler back to Maxwell. Although labor unrest plagued the industry, Plymouth sold almost 500,000 cars in 1937, a record, and 60% of them were four-door sedans like this one in front of the old hangars at historic Mitchell Field in Long Island, NY. Advanced styling for the time owed a bit to the Airflow, and included forward mounted waterfall grille, rounded fenders, swept back windshield, and built in trunk.

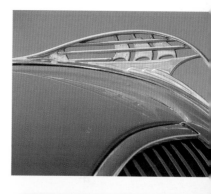

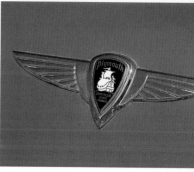

Left:
The delicate bright-work of Plymouth's waterfall grille is a legacy of the reviled Airflow Chryslers.

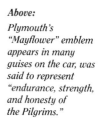

Above:
Plymouth's "Mayflower" emblem appears in many guises on the car, was said to represent "endurance, strength, and honesty of the Pilgrims."

Above:
*Retractable headlights were developed from
Stinson aircraft landing lights, and
operated by handcrank on dash.*

The Future has a Coffin Nose...1936 Cord 810/812

The prime thing about the 810 Cord's design is that it is not just an exercise in streamlining. The car has been given a personality unlike any other car before or since, by designer Gordon Beuhrig. The blind, bluff front end plows forward implacably and can still stop first time viewers in their tracks. Where's the radiator? Where are the headlights? It does not resemble those teardrop shaped "cars of the future" that adorned the covers of every popular science magazine. That coffin nose echoes the shape of the V-8 engine block beneath, and those "moderne" louvers running round front and sides are functional cooling vents. Functional also are the chromed exhaust pipes on the supercharged 812. The new front-wheel-drive Cord drew raves upon its introduction and after a few teething troubles seemed to be set for a long run. But E.L. Cord had become preoccupied with other business. He simply stopped production, first of the Duesenberg, then the Auburn and finally, in August 1937, the Cord. Only 3000 were ever made, but they pointed the way for stylists and designers for the next 10 years.

Above:

Engine-turned dash is aircraft inspired also. Tiny pre-selector gearshift is mounted on steering column.

Right:

This is the nose that changed everything; after the Cord, cars would begin to emphasize their width, using ever more horizontal grille designs.

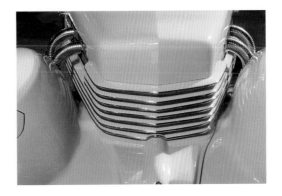

This page:

Chrysler's streamlined window layout was possibly its most agreeable looking feature, influencing other car makers up through the 1940s.

Though the Airflow design was not successful, it influenced many non-Chrysler cars including the Lincoln Zephyr and the 1937 Ford shown below.

Opposite page:

Called the "waterfall" grille for obvious reasons, the Airflow's rounded hood was a masterpiece of Deco metal working.

Overleaf:

1940 Chevrolet

GM's brand of streamlining seemed more pleasing to buyers. As the 30s progressed, Chevys got gradually lower, longer, and sleeker.

1935 Chrysler Airflow

Not so for the Chrysler Airflow. The excuse for its failure was: "It was ahead of its time." The reality was the Chrysler and its unhappy partner the DeSoto were just plain ugly. They were heavy looking and fussily decorated in an over the top deco style. A wind tunnel had shaped the car but it looked worn down by the wind rather than aggressively cutting through it as the Cord and the new Lincoln Zephyr did. While the interior layout was revolutionary and spacious, and its unit body construction really was ahead of its time, customers could not abide the Airflow and they were gradually phased out. Not until the mid 50s would Chrysler again flirt with cutting edge styling.

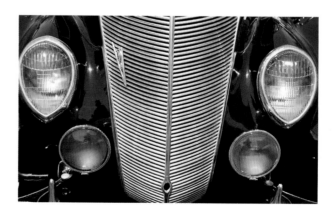

Above:

*Radical streamlining of '42 and '47
Cadillacs offended some, but didn't
stop from setting new sales records.*

Left:

*Finer eggcrate pattern of '42 grill
is shown here.*

Dreamboats...

1947 Cadillac Series 62 Club Coupe

The fastback coupe shown here is actually a '47 model, but except for its heavier grille could be a body double for the 1942 car. The entire GM line that year had been extensively streamlined. GM's "C-bodies" used on sporty models such as the Series 62 coupes and convertibles, had long teardrop fenders extending out onto the front doors and bold chrome moldings that gave a taste of things to come.

1941 Lincoln Continental Coupe

Ultimate legacy of Edsel Ford, the elegant Continental was literally the last of the Classics. Edsel asked Bob Gregorie, head of Ford styling, to design a personal auto for him, based on long light touring cars he had seen on "The Continent." Using the new Zephyr's frame, front end, and V-12 engine, Edsel's new car was such a sensation among friends in Palm Peach that the "Continental" was rushed into production. Lincoln built only about 1000 of the 1940 and '41 models; their striking proportions and luxurious appointments led to Continental being accorded full Classic status.

Below Left:

This 1941 design Cadillac retained the upright formality of classic Caddys and was used on stately Model 75s into early postwar years.

Below Right:

This 1941 model Continental, owned by a South Carolina couple, sports an original coupe body, but underneath is modern running gear from a '92 Mercury.

"The New Look"...

1948 Tucker

Preston Tucker's quixotic notion to build a totally new automobile brought cheers from those who were getting impatient for the promised new postwar cars. Could Tucker have succeeded? Congress and the SEC, in their wisdom, made the question unanswerable. The car itself seemed first rate, but though the much-ballyhooed exterior design was striking, it seemed a bit crude in execution. Noted designer Alex Tremulis' concepts, so promising in early sketches, did not adapt well to the limitations of low production techniques that Tucker was forced to adopt. Ironically, the Tucker is most radical under the skin. Engine is a rear mounted air cooled "flat-six" putting out 166 HP, highest of the day. The car was long and heavy, but performed like a racecar, and was easy on gas. Interior design focused on passenger safety.

Remembered fondly today, almost all of the 51 built still survive. The one pictured is Number 13, exhibited now at the Swigart Museum in Huntingdon, PA.

Previous pages:

This 1948 Tucker Number 13, in Walz Blue, cruises the streets of Huntingdon, PA, kept in roadworthy condition by the Swigart Museum.

Above:

Fender airscoop here is functional, unlike later Cadillac's, as Tucker engine is rear-mounted.

Right:

Swept back front-end design seems closest to original intent of Tremulis sketches.

Above:

*Rear deck of Tucker is
simple, functional. Note the
unique six-tailpipe layout.*

Right:

*Early use of fin in taillight
seems a bit "stuck-on."*

Above:
If ever a car "looked like it was going 60 when it was standing still," it was the Loewy "Bullet nose," seen here at a Studebaker show at South Street Seaport, New York City.

1950 Studebaker Four-Door Sedan

By 1950 people had gotten used to the Raymond Loewy designed "coming and going" post-war Studebaker designs. Loewy started working with Studebaker in the late 30s and helped the venerable automaker to scoop the industry by introducing the first true post-war models. Available in May 1946, their jaunty forward thrusting lines endeared them to deprived motorists. The overhead view at left shows off the "bullet nose" grille introduced in 1950 as well as the unchanged, tapered rear deck and wrap around back windows. Underneath, they were competent quality cars, with a competitive Borg Warner-engineered automatic. Record sales of over 300,000 cars were good enough for Stude to hold on to ninth place. With a new V-8 coming for 1951, Studebaker foresaw great things for its second century.

This page:

Famous designers like Raymond Loewy, and Virgil Exner, who helped create the new Studebakers, and GM's Harley Earl had mastered a brash optimistic vocabulary of product design that spilled over into consumer goods in every niche of American life as the 50s dawned.

Clockwise from top:

*1947 Buick clock;
1947 Cadillac taillight;
1947 Dodge radio.*

1948 Packard Custom Eight Victoria

Just as with the "New Look" fashions coming out of Paris in 1947, some of the new designs coming from Detroit were accepted as attractive, modern machines, and some were seen as ugly or bizarre. The new Packards, appearing in August 1947 got a mixed reception. First models to appear were the convertibles, like this Custom Eight Victoria, Packard's first ragtop since before the war. They were sleek streamlined luxury cars with appointments and trim in keeping with Packards of the past. But frankly they looked a bit rotund. Although they won awards for design, the Packard Series 22 was also ridiculed as a "pregnant elephant."

1950 Mercury Custom Convertible

Postwar Mercurys introduced in April '48 were greeted quite differently by Middle America. Yes, they were called the "Bathtub Mercs," but they were long and low and lent themselves to being "chopped and dropped" by hot rodders and customizers. The photo shows a custom Mercury with Buick headlights and a DeSoto grille.

1950 Ford

The car shown on the following two pages was actually the first of the Big Three's designs to debut. In June 1948, before any of GM or Chrysler's new models, the first all-new Ford in almost a decade rolled out. Buyers liked what they saw. Outside, the Ford's puppy-like eager to please lines emphasized its clean-slate newness. Inside was a new chassis with new suspension front and rear and a comfortable interior. Sales that first year easily topped one million.

Overleaf:

In this bucolic setting in up-state New York, a 1950 Ford convertible exhibits its simple good looks. Design was overseen by new Styling head of Ford, George Walker, with major work done by outside consultant, George Caleal.

Above:

Simple was the watchword with postwar Ford's dashboard, a far cry from the spaceship control panels of just a few years later.

Left:

The fact that James Dean drove one added immeasurably to cachet of "Bathtub Merc."

Super Cool...

1956 Chevrolet

Wow! A two-tone '56 Bel Air convertible. How cool is that? The answer is: just as cool as it was fifty years ago. This blue and white rag-top was a nicely face-lifted version of the all-new but too austere '55 model powered by the second edition of what would become a legendary engine — the small-block Chevy V-8. The Bel Air was the priciest of Chevys, GM's lowest priced car, but the 8-cylinder convertible could be had for less than $2500 in a dizzying array of two-tone color schemes. If you could afford a new car you could afford this one. By the early 21st Century all the bland gray and beige six-cylinder two-door coupes have been selected out and although these machines were seen then as basic transportation, we look upon all these colorful survivors as giant toys and shake our heads in wonder that our staid old grandparents drove cars like this every day.

Left:

All of this lovingly detailed chrome trim might seem garish to our eyes now, but by the late fifties it would seem the model of restraint.

Above:
*Best place to show off your Bel Air, then as now—at the
drive-in, the burger joint, or in front of the
pizza place—preferably with top down.*

1953 Cadillac Eldorado Sport Convertible

Certainly not your every day ride, the 1953 Eldorado was an exclusive car, easily the most expensive US car available that year, at $7750. Virtually a production version of a 1952 show car, the well-named Eldorado had the world's first "panoramic" windshield, cut down doors, and a metal "boot" covering the retracted convertible top. They were basically customized Series 62 convertibles measuring 18 and one-half feet long but looking even longer with cut down windshield and top. Only 532 people were lucky enough to acquire one. You might call it an "Eldo" to show your nonchalance around such opulence, but you'd be forgiven for losing your cool around this fiery red sport convertible. It just shouts "oil money" or "Vegas headliner" doesn't it?

Left:

Heavy conical bumper guards were called "Dagmars" after a well endowed TV hostess of the time, and became the Cadillac's trademark for most of the decade.

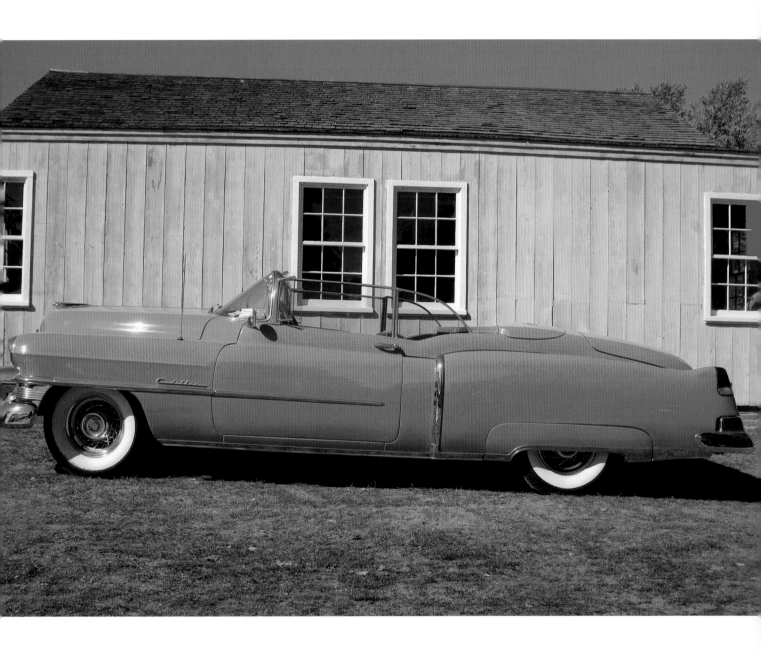

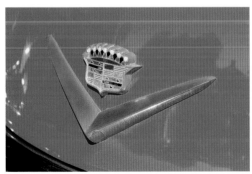

Above:

Not a Texas ranch but a shed in Bridgehampton Long Island, near the red Eldorado's home base.

Left:

Cadillac had switched to gold for its "V" hood emblem in 1952 to mark its fiftieth anniversary.

1955 / 1957 Thunderbirds

First introduced in 1955, the two-seat T'bird just about pegs the meter on cool. Ford's division manager at the time, Lewis Crusoe, thought America should have a sports car like the ones he'd seen at the Paris Auto Show and put stylist Frank Hershey to work on one. This was a purely American interpretation of the sports car, looking very trim and smooth, almost a scale model of the newly styled '55 sedans, with some touches from the X-100 concept car. Unlike the rival Corvette's no frills approach, the Thunderbird provided every creature comfort including power windows and seats. The removable hardtop shown in the photos, which was given "portholes" in '56 and '57, was factory standard, but a convertible "soft top" was optional. A bored-out version of the new overhead valve V-8, initially putting out almost 200 HP powered the T'bird, though the car was more a boulevard cruiser than a racer. Everybody wanted one. Over the three-year lifetime of the two-seater upwards of 50,000 were sold. The last year for the two-seat T'bird, was also its most popular, though Ford would go to a four seater in '58 and leave the sportscar market to GM's Corvette. The 1957 Thunderbirds were restyled, gaining fins very like those on full size Fords, and a 300 HP super-charged engine.

Left:
1956 Thunderbird featured "Continental kit" rear tire mount to increase trunk space, but handling was adversely affected by extra weight.

Above:

*Front view of '56
model seen at New
York City's first annual
Concours in 2005*

Left:

*Lower photo shows
finned 1957 T'bird, last
of the two-seaters.
Note "portholes" on
hardtops of both cars.*

1956 Ford

The Thunderbird's big brother in 1956 was this economical yet stylish family car seen at right in its sharpest looking incarnation, the Fairlane Victoria Hardtop. Some striking two tone paint schemes made the newly facelifted Hershey design the height of 50s fashion, though Ford made its first timid attempts to sell safety that year. Seatbelts, dished steering wheels, and crash-resistant doorlocks were available, but didn't seem to ignite the public's interest. On the left is what could be called the "Safety Ford's" evil twin. A teenager's dream of cool, it is also a '56 Victoria but with its flat black paint job plastered with race decals, it is sinister, powerful, and rough around the edges. The "Liberty Special" stock car racer is preserved as it was raced in the 60s with a beefed up T'bird 312 engine and full roll cage, but with most other components including transmission and brakes pretty much factory stock. A Long Island man owns both cars.

Opposite:

Race number 250, left, made the circuit of all three Long Island, NY tracks from 1963 to 1967, and though long retired, is shown today in original condition at local auto shows.

Above and right:

Ford's "checkmark" chrome trim made for dramatic two-tone color schemes in 1955 and '56 that seemed just what buyers wanted as GM and Chrysler offered similar 2-tone and even 3-tone patterns in rainbow hues.

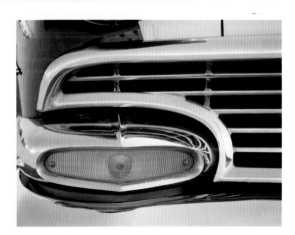

Above:

This is the lean and mean '57 Corvette, considered by most to be the epitome of the first iteration of the design.

The Ultimate American Classic...
the Corvette

Harley Earl thought his son might like a peppy little sports car at college. He put his staff of designers to work and the result was the first Corvette—developed for a GM "Motorama" show in 1952 and shown as a fiberglass prototype at the 1953 New York Auto Show. Though powered only by a 150 HP six and sitting on what was essentially a cut down sedan chassis, the machine looked great and public reaction was good. But not until the small block V-8 went under the hood of the '55 model did America's first real sports car take off. In 1957 fuel injection upped the ante with "one HP per cubic inch," shrinking 0-60 mph times to under 6 seconds, world class numbers in those days. Competition-minded America's obsession with British and Italian sports cars now had to make room for this US upstart. Famed racing engineer Zora Duntov tweaked suspension and powertrain to make Corvette a real competitor on the track. This just as Chevy and other manufacturers began de-emphasizing racing in 1958. Corvette was not helped either by all the chrome and gee-gaws typical of late 50s GM cars. In fact sales in the 50s never met expectations and it is said that only the advent of the Ford Thunderbird in 1955 spurred GM to continue production of the 'Vette. Not until 1963 with the advent of Bill Mitchell's Stingray did Corvette take off again.

Below:

Below are close ups of the 1954 Corvette showing the mini-fins on the taillights and the faux stone guards over the headlights. About one-fifth of the '54 'Vettes were delivered in Pennant Blue.

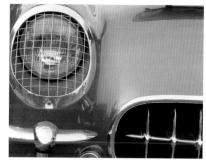

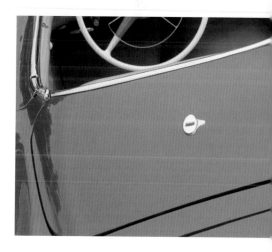

Still Unrivaled...1953 Studebaker Starliner

Above:

The basic Starliner body would soldier on in various forms for another ten years, helping keep Studebaker afloat and proving the basic soundness of the design.

1953 Studebaker Commander Starliner Hardtop

In the NY Museum of Modern Art's 1953 exhibit "Ten Automobiles," there was only one American car, the Studebaker Starliner hardtop. The car still stands as a prime example of American industrial design. Once again Raymond Loewy studios and Bob Bourke in particular gave the Studebaker Company a chance at success, but even these striking hardtops would not save the firm.

Taking cues from European touring coupes such as Cisitalia and Ferrari, and sculpting tauter curves than other American cars used, the Starliner looked faster and lower than its rivals. The design shows subtlety and restraint in every detail, including its minimal wheel covers, that lent it an elegance beyond its price range. Some minor quibbles: engine choices remained unvaried since 1951, and the sedan bodies were blockier and less sleek than the hardtops, demand for which far exceeded supply.

Above:

Front view shows aggressive new styling for 1969 with options such as: front and rear spoiler and high back front bucket seats.

Left:

Split quad headlights were unique to '69 Mustang, but have been resurrected for 2005. Hood clips were factory options.

Pony Stampede...

1969 Mustang Sportsroof GT

Looking back from the end of the 60s, Ford's Mustang could be said to have seen it all—from the 1960 Falcon that lent its chassis to the original Mustang, to the 1962 and '63 Mustang I and Mustang II show cars, to the "1964 1/2" model that was guided to production by Lee Iacocca. Its instant appeal to everyone from economy freak to performance nut spelled record-breaking sales of more than a million in two years. This really irked the competition and started a "pony car" race. Contenders were GM's Camaro and Firebird, Ford's own Mercury Cougar and even AMC's entry, the Marlin. Mustang's adaptability helped it join the muscle car brigade also—by 1969 five different V-8 engines in 8 different power set-ups tempted power junkies with the humongous Boss 429 topping the list. Lending excitement to Mustang's first five years was Steve McQueen's piloting a '68 GT-390 fastback through a wild car chase in the movie "Bullitt" and Carroll Shelby's great modified GT-350 and GT-500 Shelby-Mustangs.

The formidable looking Gulfstream Aqua 1969 Mustang in these pictures is a totally stock 351 cubic inch V-8 model GT, one of the last made before Ford introduced the Mach 1 models. This award winning all-original fastback shows the unique for '69 four-headlight front-end styling that was the inspiration for the all-new 2005 Mustang.

Below:

Triple taillights had been a Mustang trademark since the car's introduction and have remained an identifying feature in various guises until today

Hood scoop is functional though rear trim shown is merely decorative.

Right:

Red paint job and aftermarket wheels are all the warning you will get that this is one hot little Nova!

Below Right:

No self-respecting muscle car of the 60s was complete without racecar derived hood clips. Hood scoop feeds 3 2-barrel carburetors.

1967 Chevy II Nova

Even the humble Chevy II could be had with muscle car credentials; witness the Nova Super Sport 327 V-8 option pack, but the '67 Nova pictured here is a real sleeper. Under its mild mannered family car skin is a modern custom powertrain. Except for the new Boyd Coddington 17 inch low profile wheels, you'd have no clue about the 400 HP '69 Chevy 350 block with 4-barrel "Speed Demon" carb under the hood, the 700 R4 transmission, or the "12 bolt" posi-traction rear end.

1969 Plymouth Roadrunner

Totally different in approach from the mild appearing Nova was the in-your-face Roadrunner. Based on the Plymouth intermediate-sized Belvedere, the Warner Bros. animation-inspired Road Runner with its cartoon logo, wild colors, and "beep-beep" horn appealed to the "Youth Market" especially in view of its price of around $2500. Almost 40,000 sold in the first year, 1000 of them with "Street-Hemis" that could hit 130 MPH in the quarter mile. This "1969 1/2" model shown has its original 440 cubic inch engine but now has a matte black "lift-off" hood and aftermarket wheels as well as wild new paint scheme.

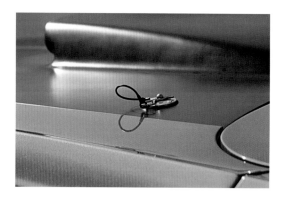

Above:

Custom Roadrunner's five color metallic paint scheme shades from light to dark copper, front to rear, with "meteor" flames running the length of the body.

77

A Doomed Masterpiece...
1963 Studebaker Sports Coupe

1963 Studebaker Avanti Sports Coupe

Studebaker in trouble—again! Raymond Loewy Studios to the rescue—again! This time Studebaker's new president, Sherwood Egbert gave Loewy little over a year to develop a prototype. Just as in 1953, Loewy turned to Europe for inspiration, using a nipped-in "coke bottle" fuselage like that on the new Jaguar XK-E, with a long hood and underslung air intake that evoked Italian GT cars. Working in Palm Springs, California, Loewy and a three-man team had a quarter-sized concept model done in two weeks, and the full-scale clay model ready for final approval in 40 days. Using a modified Lark chassis suitably tweaked for better handling, the Avanti Sports Coupe offered several performance options including a supercharger. After delays with the fiberglass body, the car premiered in late 1962 to great critical acclaim. Avanti did everything expected of it on the road but could not save the company. After building fewer than 5000 by January 1964, Studebaker moved to Canada where it managed to eke out a few more Lark based cars before leaving the auto business in 1966. Enthusiasts bought the Avanti's body molds and tools and built small quantities of the much-loved car right up until 1992.

Above:

Sensuous curves of rear deck contrast well with simple, almost severe detailing of lights and bumpers.

Left:

Not all '63 Avantis had these delicate side mirrors.

Above:

After the Studebaker's demise, enthusiasts bought the Avanti's body molds and tools and built small quantities of the much-loved car right up until 1992. However, the original Avanti had a purposeful nose-down rake that was lost in later privately built models.

Sizing Down, Powering Up...

1970-1980

Conscious of the fact that 30 years have passed, that the tinkering and tweaking goes on, that not everyone believes a car must be restored or kept in the state that it left the factory, we offer a look at some of the last of the muscle cars.

1970 Chevelle SS

This 1970 Chevelle SS is a product of 21st Century technology, though it looks almost as it did back in '70. Beneath the hood scoop and stripes, it boasts a 502 cubic inch GM F-1 engine block (developed from a boat engine), that is mated to the popular 700R4 transmission. Four-wheel disk brakes are new. Inside and outside, however the car looks just as it did when it was a stock SS 396. Back in the day, the most ferocious Chevelle was the SS 454 LS-6, with 450 HP.

1971 Nova SS

The black '71 Chevy Nova SS (does not stand for smoked salmon!) was still a sleeper, even though the top engine choice was now the 350 with "just" 245 HP. The year before, the Nova's oversize engine compartment could be stuffed with the L78 version of the 396 engine that churned out 375 HP. Still, 7000 '71 Nova SS models found buyers.

1973 'Cuda

To keep this section from becoming an all-Chevy monologue, we've included Plymouth's finest fish, the 'Cuda in one of Chrysler's "High Impact" colors, "Moulin Rouge." The all white interior with new for '73 High back bucket seats really sets off the psychedelic pink. But the legendary Hemi was gone and power was now limited to the 318 or the 340 V-8 engines.

Left:
Moulin Rouge color was not available on the '73s but owner has repainted and also removed clumsy rubber front bumper guards. Hood scoops on 'Cuda are non-functional.

Opposite page top:
Power view of Chevelle SS showing reverse-style hood scoop that drew air from a high-pressure area at base of windshield at high speed.

Opposite page bottom:
This mild mannered black coupe hides its identity except for the modest "SS" badge on trunk lid.

The Last Convetible...
the 1975 Chevrolet Caprice

Above:

*Top-down view of Caprice emphasizes car's
18-foot length as does horizontal trim and
partial rear wheel covers.*

By the mid-seventies the American auto industry began trying to deal with these new challenges: high gas prices, government regulation, increasingly popular Asian and European imports. Internal problems plagued Detroit as well: build quality deteriorated and financial problems threatened Chrysler's very existence. Expectations were diminished; sights were lowered, quite literally in the case of top-down drivers. Chevrolet built its "Last Convertible" in 1975. The car was loooong! — a rectangular dream barge — that with the new stretched out five-mph bumpers, was longer than any Cadillac, let alone Chevrolet, made today. Weighing 4300 pounds and powered by a de-tuned 145 HP engine mated to the new catalytic converter, you weren't going anywhere fast. So, be glad the seats were luxurious and your top was down. Though downsizing worked its wonders to produce more efficient four-cylinder and front wheel drive V-6 engines, these full size rear-drive cruisers wouldn't go away; all of the Big Three's low-priced marques kept them in production through the mid-80s. But ragtop fans would have to wait until 1984's Cavalier for a new Chevy Convertible.

Since the late 40s, dwellers in the alternate universe of hot rods and customs have used flame painting and striping to decorate their creations. Artists such as Von Dutch, Big Daddy Roth and George Barris resurrected the lost art of pinstriping, and took it to new, almost compulsive, levels. Flame painting started as simple red or black shapes on the front of postwar hotrods. Possibly there was some connection with the scallop shapes that were common on 30s racing airplanes. But flames had staying power, morphing into huge artworks that covered entire cars and have, if anything, gotten more popular with passing years, as seen on these pages.

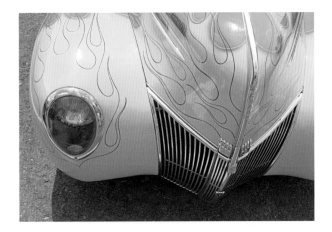

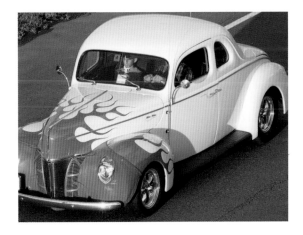

Flaming Fords

Opposite page:

A '32 Street Rod bathed in "wave curl" flames.

This page

Top:

'39 Ford DeLuxe carries both flames and stripes, with the stripes being outline flames.

Center:

'38 Ragtop in customizers' favorite color, purple, and beautifully airbrushed extended stripes.

Bottom:

1940 Ford five-window coupe with modern application of earliest form of flame painting. This scheme could have been seen on "belly-tank" racers out at Muroc Dry Lake right after WWII.

Yes, but is this an
American Car?...the 1981 DeLorean

This page:

A unique example of a rare automobile, this one is signed by Jon DeLorean himself on the driver's side doorjamb.

Though brushed stainless body cladding makes for a distinctive look, cleaning it proved labor intensive.

Even as the decade began there were some who ditched it all to follow a dream; a scenario that would become more common as the high-flying 80s climaxed. John Z. DeLorean had grabbed all the brass rings in his 17 years at GM. Now the father of the GTO wanted what even ace entrepreneur Preston Tucker couldn't have, his own auto company. This was not to be a small custom house turning out a few hand built masterpieces a year, but a full production factory with a capacity of thousands annually.

1981 DeLorean DMC-12 Sports Coupe

With sensational drawings and models from Italian designer Giorgio Giugiaro appearing in 1974 to whet investors' appetites, start up capital was no problem. The factory was to be in Northern Ireland. Though promised for 1979, deliveries were delayed until spring of '81. The car looked the part: low wedged-shaped profile, amazing gull-wing doors, stainless steel clad body. But the engine, an anemic 130 HP V-6 from France's Renault, did not excite, and sales faltered. Financial problems snowballed and even DeLorean himself faced drug charges. The company folded at the end of 1982 with only 4000 DeLoreans making it to the US. Today they are prized collectibles.

Ultra-Clean Road Machines...

On these pages:

A sampling of custom coupes and roadsters in that slick understated style popularized by the creations of Boyd Coddington and the Billy Gibbons "Eliminator" 'rod that got endless airtime in the videos of ZZ Top.

Left:

The 1940 Willys makes a very smooth 'rod if you can find one—only 20,000 of all types were made.

Left Below:

A clean-looking '33 Ford roadster heads off into the sunset. Those huge rear tires are for one thing only—running the quarter-mile.

Right:

Sometimes a Ford just won't do—this '37 Chevy coupe typifies the clean monochrome looks popularized by 80s phenomenon Boyd Coddington and others.

Left:

*Odd man out here
started as a 1986
Chevy S-10 pickup
customized for a
South Carolina man
by Master Street Rods,
sports a 350 engine
and a grille with
touches of 30s
Ford, Studebaker,
and Willys.*

Above and right:

*Riviera's pugnacious grille and
sweptback fenders minimized
apparent size of the large
sport coupe.*

Comes the Jellybean...

Wind tunnel testing to improve automotive aerodynamics started as a way to boost gas mileage in what was thought would be the fuel starved 90s. Though gas remained plentiful in those years, some remarkable cars resulted.

1994 Ford Taurus LX

The 1986 Taurus was a truly revolutionary car. Folks either loved or hated the "Jelly Bean" styling. Though the design, by Jack Telnack, was extreme enough to make a credible futuristic cop car in "Robo Cop," with a drag ratio of only 0.33, this was not the whole picture. Production techniques and inventory were modernized, quality control shaken up, interior materials and ergonomics re-thought, and chassis and drivetrain engineering made state of the art. The 1994 model pictured shows a slightly toned down design from the '86, as Ford readied its radical new 1996 Taurus. In its 10-year run the Taurus was judged a success, though Honda led in sales.

1995 Buick Riviera

Taking a much more sensuous sporty approach than the smooth but faceless Taurus, Buick's Riviera for 1995 had to live up to a spirited legacy dating back to Bill Mitchell's first 1963 design. GM's Bill Porter, using the same platform as the Olds Aurora, based his "muscular and romantic" design on the '91 Lucerne concept. A 3.8-liter engine with 240 HP gives the "Riv" some real muscle. But sales disappointed, and the Riviera nameplate has been "retired" for now.

Fantasy for the "Car Guy"...
Plymouth Prowler

1998 Plymouth Prowler

Typical of Chrysler in the 90s was the Prowler. Think of the ferocious Dodge Viper of 1992. At the time, Chrysler's president Bob Lutz and head of design Tom Gale, both avowed "car guys," had set up the Heritage Design Program. Its purpose: to troll Chrysler's past for new concepts. One such was the Prowler, the result of an idea scrawled on a 3 x 5 card at a brainstorming session for a "hot-rod style retro car." Sketches and models by Chrysler's Brian Nesbitt led to a '93 concept car that generated a major buzz. Production followed in '97. The Prowler's slick roadster styling recalls Coddington creations like his "Aluma Coupe," with the shovel nose and fat rear wheels of a highboy street rod. Lightweight aluminum is used in chassis, body and in V-6 cylinder heads. It is unlikely we'll ever see a "factory built hot rod" like this again.

Opposite page:

Beautifully detailed front end disguised problems that no other modern production car has ever had to deal with: exposed wheel geometry and cycle fenders, street legal bumpers, faired-in headlights.

Above:

Oval dashboard is homage to "Deuce Coupe" ancestors. First two years' only color choices were "Yard Deep" purple and yellow.

2000–

The Golden Age Revisited...
In Silver

Lately, America's Big Three automakers have hit some rough patches. We hope they are working on fuel efficient, alternative energy vehicles that will outdo (and outsell) the Prius, somewhat along the lines of Ford's concept "Model U" world car or GM's hydrogen powered "Sequel." But these worthy machines tend to be a mite technical and, frankly, boring. Therefore, with so many great ideas emerging from Detroit's designers and engineers, we've chosen to concentrate on those that recall the mid-century Golden Age when nothing could come close to Motor City machines. We all need a little excitement to go with our sober social responsibility. As it happens, all our choices are finished in silver, America's favorite car color, a sleek, lustrous finish that is emblematic of the future.

Top and opposite:

2004 Dodge Slingshot

The Dodge "Slingshot" concept comes closest to a "green machine;" a rear mounted 100 HP, 3 cylinder engine gives peppy performance, but fuel efficiency is paramount—typically 45mpg. It's designed to be a fun to drive entry-level sports car.

Above:

2004 Chrysler ME 4-12

Daimler Chrysler's ME 4-12 abandons the retro look they have relied on successfully lately for a futuristic state of the art super-car designed by Brian Nielander. Rumors are the 850 HP, 250 mph V-12 will see production soon.

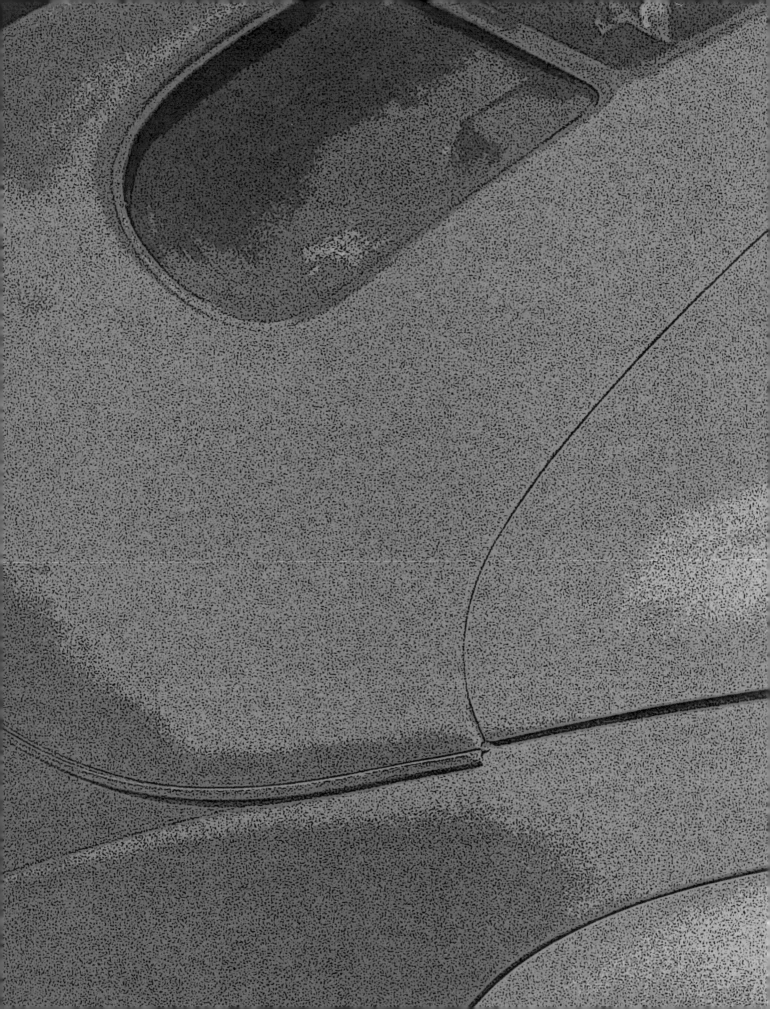